ARMED *and* DANGEROUS

From Wounded to Warrior

VANESSA MININGER

WESTBOW
PRESS®
A DIVISION OF THOMAS NELSON
& ZONDERVAN

WestBow Press books may be ordered through booksellers or by contacting:

WestBow Press
A Division of Thomas Nelson & Zondervan
1663 Liberty Drive
Bloomington, IN 47403
www.westbowpress.com
1 (866) 928-1240

ISBN: 978-1-9736-6068-2 (sc)
ISBN: 978-1-9736-6069-9 (e)

Library of Congress Control Number: 2019904812

Print information available on the last page.

WestBow Press rev. date: 04/23/2019

For my dad, who never got to read this in its published form, but never doubted that I would one day see it through to completion. Thank you for encouraging me to live my best life no matter the challenges. I miss you. Love, your Messy Nessie

Introduction

Recently a local man defaced a World War II Memorial and the outrage was widespread and justified- or so we all thought. The comment feeds from news stations across our state were full of people who called for swift justice for this "depraved individual". Some went as far as to call for his death. I'm ashamed to admit that I had some of the same thoughts. Of course I never thought that the individual should be killed, but I certainly felt they needed to answer for their crimes. A few days later the person was caught after asking a news reporter to take a picture of them in front of the defaced memorial and a witness identified him. Once he was named and his mug shot was plastered all over social media the call for action was just as intense. That is until his niece came forward and apologized for her mentally ill uncle's actions. You see, he had gone off of his medications and the family was devastated by what he had done. It was then that I no longer felt animosity towards this fellow human, but rather sympathy. I realized how quick we are to be offended without having all the facts. How we rarely look for the hurt in the offender because we are too busy being offended.

You can't go thru this life unarmed. We all have ammunition. For some it is the hurts of the past. We show off our battle scars and have put on a thick armor of self righteousness- we have gone thru the valley of the shadow of death and survived. We think to ourselves that if we survived this or that, nothing can hurt us. We protect our hearts by not opening them up to others. We don't share our thoughts, our dreams or our desires because no one can crush what they don't know. We hide behind degrees, and financial success, and powerful positions. We cry in the shower and smile in public. This world is arming itself with the weapons which only harm us and those around us; greed, lust, gluttony, laziness, wrath, envy and pride. If we are lucky we only self-destruct- but too often we take others down with us. It's time for a change. We are all armed and dangerous one way or another. We are either dangerous to the world through our wounds or through our battle to be a light in an ever darkening world. I say it's time to go from wounded to warrior.

Lust

"But I tell you that anyone who looks at a woman lustfully has already committed adultery with her in his heart"

Matthew 5:28

Sex sells. Don't believe me? Did you know that the female erotica book "Fifty Shades of Grey" sold over 100 million copies, was translated into 52 different languages, and was the fastest selling paperback book of all time in the United Kingdom? Critics and fans agree it's not well written- so why is it such a huge hit? Because sex sells- and it sells well.

Women tend to think that lust is a man's problem. A broad view of scripture seems to tout that same opinion as it generally only addresses lust in men. It warns them against the temptations of the flesh. It's well documented that the majority of women aren't as visually stimulated as men are, but the tables are starting to turn. Tawdry novels have always been big sellers with women, because women have vivid imaginations. It's much easier for us to come up with our own fantasy than it is for men. Is that why we tend to think that verses about lust don't apply to us? Because we aren't "looking"? What if the verse was reworded? What if instead it said "But I tell you that anyone who imagines a sexual encounter with another person has already committed adultery with them in their heart." Does that make you uncomfortable? It should. It made me uncomfortable to write it.

Sex can be a weapon- and a powerful one at that. In its most harmful form it is used to exert control over another person. I'm not talking about rape though. I know of too many marriages where sex is used as a weapon and never with positive results. In marriage, sex is often used as a weapon by the wife. She holds the power because she controls the system of checks and balances. A romantic encounter is only achieved if the husband has met all the requirements; are the kids in bed, are the dishes done, was he gentle and kind, do I have to get up early, are Saturn and Venus aligned? The last one is thrown in for dramatic effect, but many husbands feel that it's pretty close to this kind of checklist.

It's time for us as Christian women to stop using sex and our sexuality as a weapon. We have the power to change our marriages and influence those around us by simply refusing to use these weapons against our spouses and against each other. We could single handedly end infidelity in marriages- seriously. Affairs take two people- there are no one sided affairs. If every woman committed to respecting themselves, not just their husbands, infidelity would end. After all, if we respect ourselves, would we be willing to give ourselves over to someone who doesn't want to share every part of our lives?

Many of you reading this book have had sex used against you as a weapon. It cuts deeper than any sword and leaves scars unlike any other. Some of you have experienced molestation, rape or the pain of infidelity. As much as our culture wants us to believe that sex is just the meeting of two bodies and is just for "fun," our souls tell us different. Our deepest desire is to be loved and to feel that love expressed. God created sex to help us fill this very "fleshy" desire but we have twisted it into something that is so far from His design that it's almost unrecognizable.

In 2018 a campaign was started that had the goal of exposing exactly how many women had been a victim of sexual abuse. In theory it was a great plan- but opportunistic women turned it into a joke. Women lied to get attention, money or revenge. This destroyed the movement and instead of being an empowering platform, it became yet another example of how women use sex as a weapon just as often as men. It became the embodiment of the "Boy Who Cried Wolf" story. If one of them lied about it, are they all lying? The whole thing made me sick. For those of you who have had sex used against you as a weapon I am truly sorry for the trauma you experienced when it happened and I am even more sorry if you shared your story just to be told you were wrong for sharing it. What happened to you was wrong and there is no excuse for it- but there is healing from it, if you are willing.

Gluttony

"for drunkards and gluttons become poor, and
drowsiness clothes them in rags"

Proverbs 23:21

Do not skip this chapter because you don't struggle with this
particular vice or you don't think that it's really a sin- read through it
first and then decide. By definition, gluttony is the overconsumption
of food or drink. Who hasn't done that? Gluttony though takes it to
a whole new level, a level where food becomes an idol. We eat not
because we are hungry, but because we are trying to fill a void that
cannot be filled by food or drink. This is when it becomes gluttony.

Had a bad day? Have a drink! Eat some chocolate! What about
pray? If you told someone you'd had a bad day and they said "you
should pray about that" you would probably shoot them the evil
eye. We really don't like to be confronted with our shortcomings!
Especially when we were wanting to hear one of the first responses,
but why? Why is it that so many of us turn to wine, chocolate, ice
cream, potato chips, etc. when we have a problem instead of turning
to the One who can actually do something about it? Chocolate has
never provided a way through my problems, but God always has.

The Bible tells us the story of a gluttonous city called Sodom. I
bet you thought I would tie them to lust, but the scriptures actually

say they "were arrogant, overfed and unconcerned; they did not help the poor and needy" Ezekiel 16:49. Sounds like gluttony to me. That last part is reminiscent of our current culture- how do we have both an obesity epidemic and over 48 million Americans only being able to eat one meal a day? Did you know that the cost of dealing with the effects of obesity is $100 billion a year? That is literally enough to eradicate starvation in the entire world. Still think it's not really a sin?

We have entire television stations dedicated to our obsession with food. Most of our advertising is geared towards food and drink. You can't checkout at the grocery store without passing the racks peddling entire magazines dedicated to food! Gone are the days when we ate to live, now we live to eat!

Now don't twist my words here- I am the wife of a farmer and I love good food. I just have to wonder sometimes if we don't sometimes glorify food more than the One who provided it. I've often spent an entire day in my kitchen cooking for my family. I have never spent an entire day in God's presence praying for my family. Which leads me to my ultimate question, what good is it if I nourish my family's stomachs but starve their souls?

I believe the answer lies in balance. Make good food, but make time to thank the Lord who provided it for you and your family as well. Imagine how much better that food will taste when you eat it with your family in the knowledge that you are able to provide for your family because the Maker of Heaven and Earth provided for you.

Greed

"Having lost all sensitivity, they have given themselves over to sensuality so as to indulge in every kind of impurity, with a continual lust for more"

Ephesians 4:19

I can't hear the word greed without my mind immediately turning to Ebenezer Scrooge. He was surely the most greedy literary character whose life was changed dramatically when he was confronted with the reality of his selfish behaviors. If only we could all see the effects of our greed before it is too late.

As with most of the weapons of the world, we like to think that greed is not in our personal arsenal. We are careful, not greedy. That homeless man on the corner could just as easily go find a job. Besides, if you gave him any money, he'd probably just spend it on booze or drugs. Don't tell me you've never thought it, because I have, and it's roots are in greed.

Greed is about more than money- it's about making sure that we are comfortable. It's that voice that tells us we deserve more, better, newer, faster. If it weren't for greed, we would have no need for the advertising industry. The sole purpose of advertising is to make you think that something more is out there and you need it to be happy. That's greed- the continual lust for more.

Maybe your greed is with your time. There are only 24 hours in a day and some of us use them all to the fullest and some waste them with things that don't really matter. It's okay to be careful with your time, but don't be greedy about it. Here's a simple litmus test, if the activity you are choosing to do isn't advancing the Kingdom when you have the opportunity to do so, then you're being greedy with your time. Entertainment is good, it's healthy even, but don't miss an opportunity to serve or be fed from the Word for it. Gone are the days of saying "I can't miss my show" as an excuse- that's why God invented DVR's and Netflix. Seriously.

Maybe you aren't greedy with your time or your money. I think I'm fairly generous in both of those areas. You know where my greed lies? Power. I have a continual lust for power and control. "I want what I want, and I want it now." to quote Veruca Salt. My obsession with power isn't for my glory, it's to be in control of everything at all times. If you want to see me lose my mind, change something I thought I had under my control. There is a flip side to me though, that some find puzzling, if I'm not in control, I'm okay with whatever. Change all the plans you want. As long as you aren't messing with my power sphere, it's all good. I know how ridiculous I sound, but I'm being honest here.

When is the last time you were honest with yourself about where your major source of greed lies? Have you become complacent, or even comfortable with it? Is it your security blanket that protects you from all that is wrong in the world? Mine is. Many times I have wrapped myself up in my blanket of control and felt perfectly safe. Until it starts to stink and make me uncomfortable, because I know that true comfort doesn't come from being in control, but in knowing that I'm not.

3 Blessed be the God and Father of our Lord Jesus Christ, the Father of mercies and God of all comfort, 4 who comforts us in all our affliction, so that we may be able to comfort those who are in any affliction, with the comfort with which we ourselves are comforted by God. 2 Corinthians 1:3-4

Laziness

"The way of the sluggard is blocked with thorns, but the path of the upright is a highway"

Proverbs 15:19

I am fairly certain this chapter is the most ironic. Want to know why? Because I was too lazy to write it in the first place. I'm not even joking. I wrote EVERY OTHER CHAPTER...then returned to this one. I don't like talking about laziness because it's one of my main vices. Most people who will read this book will wonder how in the world I could possibly struggle with laziness.

I work at a Christian school full time, I'm a part time adjunct professor, I have three very active daughters, I'm the wife of a farmer and we live on an acre in the country with animals and a walnut grove. How could I possibly be lazy? Because I know the things that need to be done and instead I do what I want. I justify it in a million different ways. My favorite? "My kids are old enough that they can help out around here too." I fully believe this. I also use it as an excuse to not do dishes, clean up around the house, do laundry or cook. If I was doing anything productive during that time I could justify it, but so many times I will say "I have work to get done" only to get sucked into a television show, a Facebook story or some other distraction that has zero to do with what I was intending to do.

I use to think that it wasn't possible for me to "do nothing". I am always doing something. But if our definition of being productive is just doing "something", we have veered off the path and have began blazing our own trail of ignorant bliss.

Often, when speaking to my husband, I use farm analogies to try and help him understand what I'm trying to work through. When it comes to laziness, there are many different scenarios for the farm analogy. Jesus used them too. Let's imagine that a farmer decided that he wants to grow a crop of corn. In scenario one, he is lazy in the spring and doesn't plant the corn. That's a big problem. Very few of us want something and then don't even take the first step. Unless it's a diet. I always want to lose weight, but I rarely get past the "wanting" stage.

Scenario two: the farmer plants the corn, but he forgets to water it. The corn doesn't grow. It stays in the ground and eventually withers up and dies. A lot of us get to this point. We have the idea, we take the first big step and then once the initial excitement of starting it is gone, we quit.

Scenario three: the farmer plants the corn, waters the corn but then harvest comes and it's just too much work. So he leaves it. This sounds ridiculous doesn't it? We do it all the time though. We put in the hard work of starting and maintaining but then that last step to follow through, the one that will give us the big payoff, it's just too much...so we quit. Real life examples? How about that college degree you always said you would finish? The promotion at work that just needs you to take that last step? The home improvement project that needs just one last BIG thing? I'm calling you out. There's only one thing left for you to quit to achieve everything God has planned for you. Quit being lazy.

"... if anyone is not willing to work, then he is not to eat, either. For we hear that some among you are leading an undisciplined life, doing no work at all, but acting like busybodies. Now such persons we command and exhort in the Lord Jesus Christ to work in quiet fashion and eat their own bread." 2 Thessalonians 3:10-12

Wrath

"A gentle answer turns away wrath, but a harsh word stirs up anger"

Proverbs 15:1

It took me awhile to write this chapter. For a long time I thought this chapter would focus on my husband. How his shortcomings were the reason for my anger. Again with the justification. My husband will tell you himself that if word sparring was a sport, he would be at olympic status. A lot of us are really good at finding just the right words to stir up anger in others. Those little jabs that we sometimes say jokingly, but have a hint of truth in them. It's the truth that hurts. When your spouse makes the joke about you gaining weight. Or you joke that your child won't be getting into any colleges with the grades they have now. Or you joke that your friend's too broke to pay attention. Here's what the other end sounds like, you're fat, you're stupid, you're poor. We would never say those words to the people we love and care about, but we do... j/k.

Usually when we talk about the sin of wrath we go straight to physical wrath. That kind of anger leaves physical scars. Ones that are visible to everyone. I believe the wrath that God is referencing is mental. The anger that stirs within us and that we suppress to the deepest corners of our memory because we are good people.

Good people don't get angry, right? Good people forgive and forget. You're only partially right and that's where the anger starts. We are called by Christ to forgive. To acknowledge the pain inflicted upon us and then let the pain go. Sometimes that means letting the person that caused the pain go too. There are times Christ calls us to forgive and move forward and there are times we are to forgive and move on. There's no clear-cut answer here, though; that's where prayer has to come in. God will let you know which one is the right answer if you just take the time to ask.

I have forgiven my spouse for things others have seen as grounds for divorce. Not little things either...big things. He's also forgiven me. I am not judging those who have moved on instead of moving forward. God led them down a different path because although the sin was the same, the sinner was not. In our relationship, sin will always be a stumbling block. We have committed to each other that no matter the sin, if the sinner is repentant, the sin can and will be forgiven.

I think when we renew our vows for our 20th anniversary, which isn't that far off, we will have new vows. "We've made it through richer and poorer, through sickness and health, through the best and through the worst, until death do us part because neither of us wants to go through this again with someone else." It's not as romantic, but it's real, and that's what matters.

> *"In your anger, do not sin. Do not let the sun go down while you are still angry." Ephesians 4:26*

Envy

Wrath is fierce and anger is a flood, but who can stand before jealousy?

Proverbs 27:4

I wish… fill in the blank. We say it all the time. Or maybe you're not a wisher, maybe you're words are "if only". It's the same thing, wanting what we don't have. It's so easy to get sucked into the pattern of wishing and wanting which leads us down the path of envy. There's actually a chain of stores in my area called "Envy". They carry all the latest and most expensive styles so that they can fulfil their namesake in this consumer-driven society. I'm not huge on fashion, I wear what's comfortable and makes me feel good, so Envy isn't a store I go to very often, unless they have a killer sale, then I'll go!

My envy is most often in lifestyles. I envy those who can travel whenever they want to wherever they want. I want to do that! I want to just take off and go places I've never been to see things I've never seen! I'm actually writing this in Monterey, California on the beach because I needed to do this very thing. I needed to just go. So I did. I wanted my husband to come with me though. I wanted us to run away for a night and spend a day just the two of us. That wouldn't work, though, because of commitments he and our children had, so he told me to go on my own. Oddly enough, I've had three friends call while I'm writing telling me they wish they could have come along.

God doesn't want us to envy others. He has so much better plans for us than we do for ourselves! What if instead of envying others, you asked God to help you fill that desire? It seems so trite to say "just pray" but what if it worked? What if you asked and God answered? Now I'm not saying sit back and wait, sometimes God answers our prayers in ways we never imagined. Actually, he usually answers our prayers in ways we never imagined. He's cool like that. So pray about it. Take your requests to the Throne of the Father and then marvel at what He will do. You are His child and he delights in giving you what you desire. Give Him the chance to show you what He's capable of doing in your life!

> *"Therefore, rid yourselves of all malice and all deceit, hypocrisy, envy, and slander of every kind. Like newborn babies, crave pure spiritual milk, so that by it you may grow up in your salvation" 1 Peter 2:1-2*

Pride

"Pride goes before destruction, a haughty spirit before a fall"

Proverbs 16:18

Pride. This is where Satan places his stronghold in almost all of our lives- he whispers in our ears "you know best", and we believe him! Our pride holds us back from so much. It prevents us from telling the entire truth, it keeps our secrets locked away even if they could help unlock someone else's guilt and shame. We don't want to let anyone know that we too have fallen. What would happen if the church "got real?" If we were able to stand up and say "I have struggled with jealousy and I don't know what to do about it?" What if people could say "I looked at pornography for years, but I found help and now I want to help others." What if he then started a group open to any man who had struggled with issues of pornography? What if his wife started a group for the spouses whose pain is equal, but not as talked about? What would a church like that look like?

I can tell you what it wouldn't look like. It wouldn't look like a bunch of put together people walking out of a service the same way they came in. It wouldn't look like a perfect set list of songs that move from upbeat and lively to calm and worshipful. It wouldn't look like

19

rehearsed prayers where everyone is silent and just listening to the person at the pulpit.

I think it would look a lot more like impassioned people sharing what God is doing and has done in their lives. It would look like people so broken in their sin that they know the only hope is in Jesus. It would look like a ragtag gang of misfits that no one fits into, so much so that the inverse happens and everyone fits in! That's what a church without pride would look like. Could you go to that church? Honestly? Can you give up the "three songs/prayer/ sermon/two more songs" service for authentic fellowship with His people? If you can't, you struggle with pride.

Jesus didn't struggle with pride. He met the people where they were and loved them to where he wanted them to be. That's the opposite of pride, that's humility. That's humbleness. That's what Christ calls us to be. I'm so tired of having warm churches across this country that are used for a few hours a week (if that much) while the least of these are cold and hungry on the street. God calls us to so much more than what our pride will let us do. If we let go of the pride, we will see how much greater good God has in store.

The Armor of God

"For though we live in the world, we do not wage war as the world does. 4 The weapons we fight with are not the weapons of the world. On the contrary, they have divine power to demolish strongholds."

2 Corinthians 10:3-4

There are two rules to any successful attack- know your enemy and know your weapons. The church is failing in both of these areas. First of all, we don't know our enemy because we don't want to know. We fail to ask the real questions, like what is so appealing and attractive about the enemies' tactics? Why do people feel so comfortable with greed and jealousy and lust and pride? Why isn't the end game enough of a persuading point to draw them away from their temporary pleasures?

You've heard it said time and time again that common sense has become the least common of the senses, but why? What tactic is the enemy using to win the battle? As Christians, we know that Christ has already won the war, but why are we so complacent in losing the battles?

It comes down to two simple things, pride and arguments. All arguments start out of an emotional response. We are human, emotions are what drive us. If an argument is stopped in the emotional stage, it is fairly easy to defeat. People can and do sit down and talk out emotions. It is when reasoning is added that the argument becomes harder to defeat. In our headline-driven society, few people take the time to read an article and even fewer take the time to derive the facts from the sources. I can't tell you how many times I have read the comments section before I read the article and have been so confused by the rhetoric that I have to read the whole thing for myself! Once I've read the article I almost always ask myself how many of the commenters actually read the article and how many gave an emotional response to an inflammatory headline. I could write an entire book on how manipulative the media can be with their headlines and click-bait, but I digress.

Despite the influence of media, the truth is the truth. Maybe that is why the first piece of armor we are supposed to don is the belt of truth. But why a belt?

Truth

"Fasten the belt of truth round your waist"

Ephesians 6:14

It's hard to understand the analogy of "putting on the armor of God" without an understanding of the roles each piece played during the time period it was being written. In the Roman army, the belt was an essential piece of equipment in a soldier's overall suit of armor. Without a belt, there would be no place for a soldier to keep his sword. A soldier without a weapon is going to be fairly useless against a well-prepared enemy. In comparison, entering a battle with Satan is going to be useless if we are not knowledgeable about the truth of Jesus Christ.

A secondary function of a soldier's belt was for protection. According to the Nelson Study Bible "from the belt hung strips of leather to protect the lower body." Likewise, truth also keeps us from harm. While we often tell ourselves that it's better to not tell the <u>entire</u> truth, this is rarely for everyone's benefit. What do you do then when you're afraid that the truth will ultimately do more harm than good? The best advice I've ever been given on this subject is to ask the person "do you really want to know the answer"? If they respond affirmatively, then they must accept responsibility for what they do with the information. Your responsibility is to share truth, you cannot feel responsible for what they do with the revelation. Too many times people withhold information because they "know" how the other person is going to respond. I can honestly say that nine times out of 10, the way I thought people would respond is rarely how they actually respond. I've built up in my mind the worst possible response to justify my holding back the entire truth, this way I convince myself that it's the "right" thing to do to spare the other person from reacting in a way that they will then regret and have to ask forgiveness for. So really, I'm doing them a favor by not telling the truth. See how easy that is to reason away? I've had a lot of practice with this one, so I just make it look easy. That being said, as I've gotten older I've let people surprise me by giving them the truth and letting them be responsible for their reaction. I'm not going to lie, I've been burned by this, but in the end I had set myself free from guilt and that made it easier to tell the truth the next time.

Don't misunderstand what I am saying, though; truth is truth regardless of opinion. Facts are truth, our feeling and opinions make up what is usually called "your truth". This is a new term that many are embracing because it frees them to make statements that are contradictory to God's word because everyone's "truth" can be different. The only truth there is is God's Truth, and truthfully, that's the only one that matters.

How do you discern the difference between "your truth" and God's Truth? It's simple, open the Bible. If you believe that the Bible is the inspired word of God, and that God only speaks the truth, then there is your paramount litmus test. Do my thoughts line up with the Word of God? I get so tired of people claiming that "God is on our side". That should not be our concern. I honestly don't think God takes sides, I think we need to concern ourselves with whether *WE* are on God's side.

Have you ever tried to walk quickly in a long skirt? It's hard! Generally if you want to move quickly, you need to take long strides. The Roman soldiers knew this well and it is why they would gather up (gird) the long ends of their robes by tucking them into their belts. Likewise, Jesus doesn't want us constricted to small steps either; so gird up those skirts, ladies and gentlemen, and prepare for battle!

As we shed the unwanted pounds that have been weighing us down: greed, envy, lust, jealousy and more, the belt becomes even more vital! Without the belt of truth, we will be swayed like the changing winds. We live in a society where there is no truth. We have bought into the lie that good and bad are relative. Social media is full of people that claim "if you don't like it, don't do it." This is a slippery slope- where do you stop? If you don't like murder, don't murder? If you don't like rape, don't rape people? These are all justifications for behavior they know is wrong but don't want to admit to the consequences of their choices. So instead they make everyone else feel guilty for "judging" them. If you're someone who uses that line, I'm not judging you, I'm praying for you, because you've got it all wrong. If you only take away one lesson from this chapter, let it be this, God's truth has never been influenced by human opinion. **AMEN.**

Righteousness

"For he put on righteousness as a breastplate, and a
helmet of salvation upon his head"

Isaiah 59:17

I had to do a lot of research to write this section. I wasn't sure what
the function was of the different pieces of armor, especially the
breastplate. It's not a weapon. It's not an offensive tool. It's merely
defensive. It protects our heart. It protects us from what would be
certain death if we were in an actual battle. That's what righteousness
does. Righteousness is not something we are supposed to use as a
weapon, but how many times do we hear people being accused of
being "righteous"? That's because the world has warped our sense
of what righteousness is and what it is not. Being righteous is about
doing right in the eyes of God.

What is right in God's eyes? The Sunday school answer is
Micah 6:8 "to act justly, to love mercy and walk humbly with your
God." That seems so simple though. Who doesn't want to act justly?
Who doesn't love mercy? Is there any choice other than to walk
humbly with God? Then we actually apply what that looks like in
our everyday life.

Act justly- In the parable of the sheep and the goats in Matthew
25 Jesus separates the people into two groups, sheep and goats.

The sheep are the people who have acted justly. The sheep are the ones who fed the hungry, gave water to the thirsty, invited in a stranger, clothed the naked, healed the sick and visited prisoners. Jesus goes so far as to say that those who did those things "for the least of these" they did for Him. The goats then have the audacity to ask "when did we see you hungry, or thirsty, or naked, or a stranger, or a prisoner?" Jesus answers the same way, if you didn't do it for the least of these, you didn't do it for me. Sure does make that homeless man on the corner look a lot more like Jesus than most of us are comfortable with, because who wants to be accused of ignoring Jesus? I'm guessing that more often than not, we have more in common with those dumb goats than we do with the sheep.

Love mercy- of course we love mercy! As a fallen people we are big fans of mercy. I know I am at least. I mess up all the time and if it weren't for mercy I'd be divorced, unemployed, estranged from my children and very possibly in jail (that's a story for another time...) Here's my problem with mercy, and probably your problem too, I don't like giving it. Sure, there are times I happily extend mercy because the person shows remorse for their actions and it would be wrong for me to not extend the same grace I have been given. The harder part is the same problem most of us have with forgiveness, when the person who wants mercy doesn't want to take responsibility for their actions. Now we've got a whole new ballgame. How are we supposed to show mercy to someone who isn't even showing us respect? Let me be completely honest here, I'm bad at this. I am like Paul, I know what I am supposed to do, but I do the opposite. I know that God showed me mercy and that I have been instructed to extend that same mercy to others in Ephesians 4:32. Simply put, mercy means that you do not condemn a person for their wrongdoing. However, showing mercy is not choosing to forget what the other person has done, to completely trust them, to let go of anger, or to feel good. Rarely is any of this easy. This is why we need to surround ourselves with a body of believers- people that will encourage us to show mercy to those we don't feel are worthy of our mercy and forgiveness. We can argue with ourselves and even with God about our reasons for not extending mercy, but when we are held accountable by others our focus often shifts and allows us to view mercy in a new light.

This is what makes up the breastplate of righteousness- doing justly and loving mercy; one shows our heart and one protects it. When we do those two things, it's impossible not to walk humbly with our God.

Here's the thing I find the most interesting about the breastplate- it didn't offer protection to a person's back. It was assumed that a soldier in battle would not turn their back and retreat. In the same way, we are expected to stand firm and never retreat from a spiritual battle. We are promised that if we stand firm, God will fight the battle for us. As hard as it may be, never turn your back on a battle for what is right.

Gospel of Peace

"How beautiful upon the mountains are the feet of him that brings good tidings, that publish peace; that bring good tidings of great things, that publish salvation"-

Isaiah 52:7

When I was younger I had no problem walking on dirt roads, through the grass, on hot sidewalks; running around barefoot was one of my favorite things. As I got older my feet became more tender and now I can barely stand a foot massage! I am on my feet a lot, so my shoes are important to me. No longer can I buy $1 flip flops. No, my feet demand Sanuks, sandals made out of recycled yoga mats that set me back $40 a pair! In my shoes I can walk on otherwise painful terrain without worrying about injuring my delicate tootsies.

In scripture, Paul refers to the shoes of "the preparation of the gospel of peace." That always confused me. How do shoes prepare me to spread the gospel of peace? Here's the thing, I was focusing on the wrong emphasis. I was trying to figure out what shoes had to do with telling people about Jesus, but what Paul wanted us to focus on was the preparing. When we prepare for something we study, we practice, we learn everything we can about a subject so that we can be successful. That's what Paul wanted us to do. He wanted us to understand that the shoes were important because they allowed us to spread the good news to everyone without fear.

Let me draw a mental picture for you. Imagine a soldier fully geared up, but barefoot. It doesn't matter if he's a 1st century Roman soldier or a 21st century American soldier. Either way they would be hard pressed to win a battle without appropriate footwear. In Paul's analogy, he compares this essential piece of armor to the importance of being prepared to share the good news of Jesus Christ with others because it is equally important as a soldier's shoes. What's the point of going to battle if you're just going to stand there? Sure, you can defend your territory, but for how long? God does not call us to be on the defensive. He calls us to move. He calls us to go out. He calls us to battle.

Faith

Have you ever seen the Disney movie "Sleeping Beauty"? There's this part in it when the Prince is trying to get to Aurora (yes, that's her name, not Sleeping Beauty) and he's having to fight his way through a thicket of thorns. He's got this huge shield that never really made sense to me- it seemed like it was just too cumbersome. However, when he makes it through the thicket and is up against the fire breathing dragon, it makes sense why he needed such a large shield. If he had a smaller shield, the fire from the dragons breath would have enveloped him; instead, it was deflected and left him unscathed.

In Biblical times, a knight's shield was his primary defense against any enemy. Having a shield that completely protected them was necessary, much like the body armor of today. These types of shields could be used to protect them from the flaming arrows shot at them from the walls surrounding a village. Without these enormous shields, they would be vulnerable. The small shields carried into combat aren't nearly as effective as the full shields meant for protection.

If you think about it, this type of a shield is the perfect analogy for faith. The purpose of a shield is to protect a person from harm. The purpose of faith is to protect us from the "flaming arrows of the evil one."

I don't believe the devil is out to get just one person at one time-that's not his end game and he's not that powerful. His power lies in being able to deceive the masses all at once. That's why the body of Christ must all raise their shields together to create an impenetrable fortress. Standing together against evil and injustice, we can make a difference. We just need to have faith.

Salvation

Helmet of Salvation- Ephesians 6:17

The helmet was the last piece of armor a soldier put on, for obvious reasons. However, last is not least. The helmet protects a soldier's most vulnerable appendage, their head! A blow to the head almost guaranteed death. If a soldier was knocked unconscious they were susceptible to any attack. If their eyes were damaged in battle they were at a severe disadvantage to their opponent. Then, of course, there was the whole risk of beheading...but let's not go there.

In our lives, we run these same risks on a daily basis. We are knocked off balance by blows to the head, usually figuratively. Your co-worker got the promotion for which you'd been working tirelessly. Your significant other makes a comment that makes you feel like a failure. Your best friend isn't returning your calls or texts and you don't know why. The doctor called and asked you to come in and discuss your results in person. Each of these can knock us off balance, some off our feet completely.

Enter the helmet of salvation- it doesn't mean we won't feel anything, but it does mean we will survive. Our salvation assures us that no matter what may happen, it's all going to be okay. That promotion you missed out on? It would have meant more time away from your family and more stress. The comment from your significant other? They will never see you the way God sees you, completely amazing and fully loved. Unsure of your friendship status? God isn't. He loves you and hears everything you have to say. Remember that people come into our lives for a reason, a season or a lifetime! Facing the possibility of death? In Christ we are promised eternal life. In the end, that's what our salvation is all about; the promise of no more pain, no more tears and no more suffering. Only God and the salvation He offers us through His Son, Jesus Christ, can offer that level of protection. If you haven't put on the helmet of salvation by accepting Jesus as your Lord and Savior, please do it now. It's the last piece of armor you need to put on- but it's the one that matters the most.

Spirit

Sword of the Spirit- Ephesians 6:17

You may have been wondering, where's the sword? What kind of soldier doesn't have a weapon? Here's the thing about weapons- they only work if you know how to use them. During the debates on gun legislation there was a commentary on how guns have never killed anyone, and that's completely accurate. A gun is completely harmless when it's not in the hands of a human. You can set it on a table, you can put it outside, you can even sleep with it under your pillow and it will never kill anyone! Enter humans- now it's dangerous. The sword of the Spirit, which is the Word of God, is the same way. You can have a Bible in every room in your house, if you don't know what's in it and how to use it, it's as ineffective as any other physical weapon in your arsenal.

Hebrews 4:12 explains: "For the word of God is living and powerful, and sharper than any two-edged sword, piercing even to the division of soul and spirit, and of joints and marrow, and is a discerner of the thoughts and intents of the heart."

Jesus used the Word of God to defeat Satan in Matthew 4:1-10. He had been alone in the wilderness fasting for 40 days when Satan appeared and tried to trick Him into turning stones into bread. Jesus simply responded that 'man shall not live by bread alone', a scripture written nearly 700 years before in the book of Deuteronomy. He knew the Word of His Father and knew how to use it. So Satan tried again and again, but each time, Jesus rebuked him with scripture. Scripture can do the same thing for us if we know it.

Have you been tempted by someone to "cover for them"? 1 Corinthians 15:33

Have you been tempted to speak ill of someone? Ephesians 4:29

Have you been tempted to spread gossip? Exodus 23:1

Have you been tempted to tell a "white lie"? Psalm 34:14

Every single problem we will ever encounter in our lives has an answer in scripture, honestly! If we take the time to read His word and commit it to memory, we will be able to face any and all problems that may come our way with the confidence that comes from a right relationship with God.

From Wounded to Warrior

It took me three years to write this book. Yep, three years to write this short little thing. I had a lot of bursts of creative energy where I would write entire sections at a time and then literally months of nothing. I would write pages at a time just to go back and delete them because they weren't good enough, in my opinion. So many times as I was writing I felt like the words weren't my own, they were coming from somewhere else, from someone else. I would think about the people who would be reading these words and wonder if what I was writing was going to make sense to them. If they would feel like this was written to them, for their eyes only. Not everything in here is from my personal life experiences, it is from the experiences of being a mom, a wife, a teacher, a friend, a daughter, a sister and a child of God. We share in many of these experiences because they are part of a life LIVED! When I pass on from this life I want it to be a testimony to the power of God's grace and mercy. I have not lived perfectly, but because of His perfect love, I have the hope of a life eternal.

> *Finally, be strong in the Lord and in his mighty power. Put on the full armor of God, so that you can take your stand against the devil's schemes. For our struggle is not against flesh and blood, but against the rulers, against the authorities, against the powers of this dark world and against the spiritual forces of evil in the heavenly realms.*

Therefore put on the full armor of God, so that when the day of evil comes, you may be able to stand your ground, and after you have done everything, to stand. Stand firm then, with the belt of truth buckled around your waist, with the breastplate of righteousness in place, and with your feet fitted with the readiness that comes from the gospel of peace. In addition to all this, take up the shield of faith, with which you can extinguish all the flaming arrows of the evil one. Take the helmet of salvation and the sword of the Spirit, which is the word of God. **Ephesians 6:10-17**

Shalom my friends.

Printed and bound by PG in the USA